# WEALTH IS NOT ABOUT THE MONEY

*The 10 Laws of Conditionomics*

*How couples integrate and grow
their personal, professional
and financial lives.*

**Michael A. Campbell**

authorHOUSE™

1663 LIBERTY DRIVE, SUITE 200
BLOOMINGTON, INDIANA 47403
(800) 839-8640
WWW.AUTHORHOUSE.COM

*First published by AuthorHouse 09/30/05*

*ISBN: 1-4208-8380-1 (sc)*
*ISBN: 1-4208-8379-8 (dj)*

*Printed in the United States of America*
*Bloomington, Indiana*

*This book is printed on acid-free paper.*

*Wealth is not about the money,
it is about the purpose for
which it is created.*

*"We live in a culture that absolutely requires substantial financial resources to achieve personal freedom and self-determination. If this is your goal, you must master the creation and application of wealth. At The Conditionomics Coach™, helping clients confidently achieve that goal is our purpose and our mission."*

*- Michael A. Campbell*
*Conditionomics Founder and President*

# Message from the Author

Did you know that less than 10% of the people who purchase a book actually read it? Your simple act of reading a book places you among a very special group of individuals who have the winning edge. As a reader, you have the advantage of shared wisdom that, when applied, accelerates progress and enables you to experience so much more of what life has to offer.

Like you, this book is different from most others. First of all it is short and to the point and second it was written for the minority of the public not the majority; those who have a passion for excellence in all three areas of life: personal, professional and financial. It is a summary of the lessons I have learned about living life based on my own personal experience and that of the many couples I have worked with over the years. These are couples like you, who are committed to growing together not apart. These are couples who, despite their efforts, are frustrated with their inability to have it all: personally, professionally and financially. These are couples who are tired of living a life of sacrifice and tradeoffs only to be disappointed in the end - couples who despite these challenges, are unwilling to give up on their dreams.

I have titled these lessons The 10 Laws of Conditionomics and written this book with one objective in mind: to help aspiring couples achieve more of the things they value in life sooner.

On behalf of The Conditionomics Coach, LLC, our members and licensed coaches, I sincerely hope you enjoy and perhaps even embrace, The 10 Laws of Conditionomics.

# CONTENTS

**Dedicated to my wife Diane,
my best friend, my soul mate,
the love of my life.**

# THE 10 LAWS OF CONDITIONOMICS

1. Happiness is achieved by integrating - not separating - your personal, professional and financial lives.

2. Life is all about achieving more of the things you value sooner – not later.

3. You will only do more if your confidence in your future increases.

4. Personal freedom and self-determination require financial success.

5. Financial success requires special "conditioning."

6.  Wealth is not about the money; it is about the purpose for which it is created.

7.  Wealth is driven by process, not transactions.

8.  Effective goal setting requires a "change of environment."

9.  A fulfilled life comes from an ever expanding view of possibilities.

10. The easiest and most enjoyable way to realize your potential is with the guidance of a skilled coach.

# PROLOGUE

I look around at my contemporaries and I am concerned. So many of them are profoundly unhappy in their present situation and pessimistic about their future.

There is a growing "crisis of confidence" in this country among people in their 40s and 50s who, from an outsider's perspective, would be considered quite successful and even affluent. These people are worried and disillusioned. Are they worried that they'll die young? No. People are worried that they'll outlive their money! Despite the fact that they have worked hard and "followed all the rules" they feel as though they haven't achieved enough and never will. Discouraged and disillusioned, they begin to spend more and more time reflecting on the past -- a time when things were good -- filled with hope and confidence – back to their youth. So they buy things or behave in ways that make them feel

1

like they can recapture that time – that feeling – when anything and everything was possible.

A few years ago I had the opportunity to cash out of the business I had built and operated for 13 years. I was excited to think about what I would do next. For years I thought that if ever the chance presented itself, I would like to share with others the lessons I learned that have enabled me to live an extraordinarily enriched and enjoyable life – one that is focused on always making the most of today while also looking to the future filled with hope and confidence.

A successful life, I discovered, isn't defined by a specific amount of leisure time or money. Each one of us has a different definition of those things. I define a successful life in terms of personal freedom and self-determination.  In other words, the most important things to me are the ability to choose what I do, and where and with whom I do it.

I learned early in my life that such freedom doesn't come cheap; so the question became "how will I achieve it?" Most people believe that accumulated wealth is achieved through personal sacrifices and financial risks. But I have found a way to have unwavering confidence in my ability to continue to earn a substantial income while doing the things I love to do right now and enjoying abundant leisure time to spend as I wish.

For me, a successful life also includes having a loving relationship with my spouse and being able to share our values, our confidence in our selves and in each other and an expanding view of the possibilities of our future together.

Using life-integrating strategies that have allowed me to achieve more of the things I value sooner, I believed that I could show others how to live an enriched and successful life -- a life filled with confidence and certainty -- a personal, professional and financial life that is balanced and integrated. This was the genesis of Conditionomics[1]. I passionately believed that if I could do it – anyone who shared my values could do it too. Those values are great love of family, personal integrity, commitment to ongoing personal development, quality of life and an open mind.

This book and the lessons within it are dedicated to those couples who share these values with each other. But before we get to those lessons, we need to shed certain "conventional wisdom."

---

[1] Conditionomics LLC is the name of the company I founded in 2001, within which I created The Conditionomics Coach Program for financial advisors.

# Are you one of the 15%?

I have a theory about why so many highly educated, ambitious, seemingly successful people are doomed to a life of financial struggle and scarcity, only to have their personal lives fall apart in middle age. It's because they are in the top 15% of the American population in terms of earning capacity but have been listening to conventional wisdom that applies to the 85% who are failing financially or barely getting by.

For the other 85% of the American population, conventional strategies sometimes work satisfactorily. But for the 15% of those committed to living long and fulfilled lives, a different kind of "economic conditioning" is needed. Following conventional rules will only lead to discontent and disillusionment.

On the road to the wrong utopia, many become alienated from their spouses and children. Why? One reason is because very few can retire when they're 65 and expect to have enough accumulated wealth to last for the rest of their lives. This is downright depressing. It's no wonder people start to have a sense of hopelessness in middle age. Especially if what they are doing for a living is strictly working for the money.

I believe this is one of the chief reasons for a divorce rate that exceeds 50% – a statistic which doesn't take into account the many couples that stay together out of convenience. Over one half of us can't be marrying the wrong person, so what is happening to us? And more importantly, what can we do about it?

## You're going to live to be 100!

If you thought you would live well into your 70s because you love your work, you have close family relationships, you have healthy living habits and you are optimistic and forward thinking – I have news for you. You're probably going to live to be 100! If you doubt this, remember that at the turn of the 19th century, a typical life expectancy was in the 40s. Notice how many people are living into their 90s these days. And consider that ever-improving healthcare and technological advances are increasing the prospects for a longer life in every generation.

Great, you say. But what will you do with the last quarter of your life? Will you be healthy, standing tall, active and living life to the fullest? Will you live in a comfortable environment? Will you have the money to travel and do all the things you want to do?

If you are still together as a couple -- if you feel as though you are constantly postponing joy – if you put off the things you enjoy doing and sacrifice time with the people you love in order to earn more money now to do those things later – you need to consider The 10 Laws of Conditionomics.

# CONDITIONOMICS LAW #1

**Happiness is achieved by integrating – not separating – your personal, professional and financial lives.**

At Conditionomics, we coach couples. We do this because it is within the concept of being "a couple" that the problem both begins and can be solved. When couples first come to us, they see their lives as being made up of three separate lives: ***a personal life*** that consists of them as individuals, their family, their loved ones and the community that they live in; ***a professional life*** that consists of them as career individuals, their business or the company that they work for, their clients and business associates; and ***a financial life*** that consists of their income, assets, liabilities and various protection instruments like insurances, wills and trusts and so on.

Society has taught us that life is all about trade-offs and sacrifices. We've been told that we have to compartmentalize our personal and professional lives, sacrificing our personal happiness now for career advancement in order to support our families and enjoy the fruits of our labors later.

As soon as two people become a married couple, they begin to separate the three aspects of their lives. They begin to delegate roles and as a result, they immediately begin to grow apart. They communicate less and less with each other about their hopes, their dreams and the larger purpose of their lives and instead, focus on mundane, everyday tasks. This continues until one day they wake up and realize they don't have much in common anymore – often leading to alienation and possibly to divorce. The question is, was that necessary? In our culture we're taught that you must divide and assign duties, responsibilities and roles in a marriage. That, we are instructed, is how you live life as a couple – how you ensure that you will have a long and happy marriage. In my experience, this is the furthest thing from the truth. I have discovered that our personal, professional and financial lives are completely **interdependent**. You can't have the best possible personal life without a great professional life. You can't have the best possible professional life without a great personal life. You can't have the best possible financial life without a great professional and personal life.

In our culture you typically grow up, living at home until at least your late teens and then go to college. Your first lesson as a young adult is that if you go to college, work hard, earn good grades and follow the rules, you'll graduate and 'Corporate America' will be sitting out there waiting to offer you tremendous opportunities. When you hit the road and interview for jobs, the companies tell you that if you come to work for them and dedicate yourself to the success of the company, they're going to compensate you well, give you tremendous opportunities for advancement and take care of you by providing insurance benefits and a retirement plan. You just have to work really hard and make that sacrifice.

# Nothing is as it was supposed to be.

So, you take the job and time goes by. You get married. You start having children. Now you have a family and you have a job, but you can't be there with the family as much as you'd like because you have to work hard for the security and benefits. So you do that. You're earning money and you have some surplus and all of a sudden the financial world wakes up to your good fortune and makes you an offer you can't refuse. They say if you give us your money today, add to it on a consistent basis and let us hold on to it for the "long term" we will create wealth and financial security for you and your family's future. If you want to be successful financially, you must make sacrifices. You can't take that "dream" vacation now; you can't have those wonderful experiences just yet – instead you must accumulate money for a safe and secure future. So more time goes by -- you are now in your 40s or 50s. Then it happens. You wake up one day and realize that you've lost touch with your spouse and you don't know your children because you haven't spent enough time with them. Lo and behold, you discover that the company you are working for hasn't been operating efficiently and the jobs are disappearing. In some cases even the pension plan has vanished. You've become more "expensive" and younger people will take your job for less, so you're not as attractive to an employer who is focused on quarterly results and shareholder value instead of long-term knowledge retention. In your financial life, you've been giving your money to financial advisors who have focused on going for the maximum return but instead have lost 25 to 40% of your wealth due to "so-called" market conditions. Nothing is as it was supposed to be. You're unfulfilled in the present; you have no future to look forward to, so you turn to the past. Some of you look back to a time when you were innocent and naïve, a time when you felt good about yourself. You buy a classic car, get in touch with old friends and perhaps start to develop bad habits that ultimately lead to divorce. You redirect the passion you once had for each other and your future together to things that are just momentary escapes.

But it doesn't have to be this way. You can recapture the hope and promise you felt when you and your spouse were dating – when you shared your visions with each other for the future and took the first tentative steps toward "couplehood." That was a time when your career possibilities seemed limitless and you were bursting with thoughts of how great it could be to share it all with each other. You were not consumed by the daily chores of living then, and you shouldn't be now. So what needs to happen?

You need to change your perspective. Understand that the ways of the past don't work. You need to look for better ways. Most importantly, from the very beginning as a couple, you need to work together to understand that your personal, professional and financial lives are interdependent. And that your personal and professional lives, not your financial lives, define who you are -- your purpose for being -- and are represented by your goals. In other words, using your values as your guide, you and your spouse, **as a team**, must cultivate and nourish goals that integrate – not separate – your lives together. But understand that this cannot and will not ever happen unless and until you rid yourselves of the myths of conventional wisdom.

## Myth #1 – The market will make you rich.

One myth that must be dispelled is that we create our wealth by investing in the stock market. I have never known anyone who became wealthy investing in the market. The fact is, we create wealth in our professional lives. What is wealth? It is the surplus income created through our work. It is what is left over after supporting our personal lives. Conventional wisdom tells us to seek a financial advisor to invest this surplus in the market to create wealth. But ***the market is not for creating wealth; it is for protecting wealth.*** That's right, its primary function is to provide a means of protecting the wealth we create in our professional lives ***against the forces that could erode or destroy it, namely: inflation, taxes, market volatility and lawsuits.*** Which means, the primary function of financial advisors is not to help us create wealth but rather to serve as custodians or protectors of our wealth.

Unfortunately most people don't believe they can create enough wealth in their professional lives, so they become vulnerable to the suggestion that "high risk" investments are a reasonable way to get "high reward." Risky investments most often lead to loss and are completely counter to what investments are for – protection.

## Myth # 2 – You must have financial goals.

Another myth offered by conventional wisdom is that you must have financial goals. ***There are no financial goals; there are only financial objectives that support your personal and professional goals.*** Money is only relevant to the extent that it serves a purpose – your purpose in life, both present and future. Many financial advisors will ask you, "How much money will you need to live on once you retire?" In other words, "How much money do you think you'll need to pay your bills every month?" Is your answer to be based on your present lifestyle or the lifestyle you will be living at the time you retire? I can tell you from personal experience, that 20 years ago I could not even imagine living the lifestyle I have today. Focusing on how many dollars you will need to maintain your current lifestyle automatically limits your view of the future. That approach will find you sitting in your rocking chair on your porch, waiting for the end of your life and hoping you won't outlive your money. What a depressing way to plan your future!

## The painful truth

One of the greatest myths of conventional wisdom is the so-called "golden years" of retirement. If we are going to live to be 100 years of age, the vast majority of the population is never going to be able to create enough wealth by age 65 to support themselves for another 35 years without continuing to work. If they want to have any kind of lifestyle, any kind of purpose, any kind of meaning, satisfaction or fulfillment, they are never going to be able to quit working. Therefore, the key to having a great life is to accept the fact that you're going to work for the rest of your healthy life. That is a very painful thought for most people; painful only because they don't like what they're doing for a living.

---

## In the future, an individual career portfolio will be commonplace.

---

The idea of lifetime employment is not new. In fact, the present day concept of retirement didn't exist until the early 1900s when the number of young workers entering the workforce far exceeded the number of available jobs. At that time the government introduced the concept of retiring at age 65 which led to the introduction of pension plans and entitlement programs such as social security, removing older workers from the workforce and freeing up jobs for the growing number of young workers.

I predict that in the years to come, the concept of ***career portfolios*** will become commonplace. People will take stock of the skills they've acquired and figure out how they can apply those skills to create value for others. They will figure out how to package and offer their skills to the market. For those of you in the top 15%, this will become a way of life. The key to having a great life, from beginning to end, is to find the things you're really good at and are passionate about and make those your work. If you can do that, then the picture turns 180° and you would be very sad indeed if you were forced to retire at 65 and never be able to do your work again.

# CONDITIONOMICS LAW #2

**Life is all about achieving
more of the things you
value sooner – not later.**

Conditionomics teaches couples life-integrating strategies for achieving more of the things they value sooner – not later. Why is this mindset so difficult to understand and to accept? At 18 or 19, many young people have the right idea – they know what they love to do. They would spend more time doing it if it weren't for parents, teachers and other well-meaning influencers in their lives who think they are giving the right advice by suggesting an education or a career with "more earning potential" or "more prestige" or "more security."

## Life's Greatest Lesson

But being a teenager is complicated in so many ways. Most people that age are supremely self-centered. And though they may think about what they love to do, they don't always make the connection to how that ability, once nurtured and developed, can create value for others. And neither do the well-meaning people around them – the ones offering the advice that makes these teenagers feel that pursuing what they love to do is selfish and wrong-thinking, even unproductive.

When I was 19, I found myself along with too many other young men, arriving in a small country in

Southeast Asia called Vietnam. As a young Marine I was about to learn life's greatest lesson, a lesson that most others learn much later in life – if at all. I learned that life is a gift and that every day and every person is precious. But the price of the lesson was high. Within just days of my arrival, I lost my best friend, was seriously wounded and then spent months in the hospital recovering with other young men who had survived the horrors of war. Many of them had lost arms and legs along with their hopes and dreams.

Most of them went home with a sense of anger and bitterness, but I was infused with a profound sense of how priceless life is and committed myself to living it to the fullest.

This perspective towards life, more than any other, has guided me and contributed to my happiness.

## The only question you ever have to ask yourself

Norman Vincent Peale wrote something to the effect that if you ever want to evaluate a decision or option before you, imagine yourself sitting in a rocking chair at the end of your life and ask yourself if you would regret having done it or not having done it. This is the only question you ever have to ask yourself. And ironically it is the easiest one to answer. Why? Because the answer expresses who you are and why you are here. So recognize that life is short and precious and when faced with important decisions simply take the rocking chair test. People should aggressively pursue the things they value in life as soon as they can and not put them off because you never know how much time you have.

## Life is about sacrifice and tradeoff – or is it?

Our culture and our society teach us that in order to get what you really want out of life you have to sacrifice and make tradeoffs. While this may be true sometimes, it also can become a perpetual habit, an embedded way of thinking, instead of an occasional "true" obstacle.

People put off the things they would most enjoy doing in the name of their future well-being. This is demoralizing and de-motivating. In the area of personal finances, this is most evident. Why? -- Because we live in a society where everything, even water, costs money. So everybody is very money-conscious. Everything is related and evaluated based on how much it costs. Even the top 15% earners don't think they have enough to live the life they want to live. So they sacrifice and trade today for an uncertain tomorrow.

If you accept that your financial security comes from your own ability to create value for others – and if you understand how to maximize that capability – you need only prepare for the bad things that can prevent you from doing that. I believe that the only true roadblock to creating value for others is a disruption or crisis in your own mental or physical health. Therefore, if you want to confidently achieve more of the things you value in life sooner, you need only prepare for this possibility. And always remember, as part of a couple, you are no longer just responsible for yourself. As such, if anything happens to you, it now affects someone else or if you have children, several others. So if you want to feel secure about the future in order to liberate yourself in the present, simply prepare so that if something happens to you, mentally or physically, then financially you and those you love will be OK – just as OK – at least financially, as if the problem had never occurred.

## Emotional well-being – the key to building wealth

Looked at another way, the key to Law #2 can be thought of as emotional well-being. Let's say you're fine mentally and physically, but you have a chronic fear or sense of hopelessness about the future. This stems from your lack of understanding about where your security comes from, believing that it comes from external sources like your employer or the stock market. I, on the other hand, believe that no matter what happens to me financially, if the market collapsed, if I lost everything, I would still be OK. I would be OK because I would retain my ability to create value for others and thereby earn the income necessary to support myself and those I care about.

## Life is graded on a curve.

Years of experience have taught me that life in our society is graded on a curve. Much the same as in college where you're graded relative to other students, as a working adult you are "graded" relative to other working adults. If you apply yourself with the right attitude and perspective, you will excel.

It's all about value creation. The United States leads the world in value creation. And as a member of this society, using your dedication, identifying and focusing on your own unique abilities, you will always have the means to support yourself and those you care about. If you have that perspective, you will have an enduring sense of confidence and hope. Don't make the mistake too many other people make. Don't look for a company or the market to provide your security. The reality is that any particular corporation or the market in general is unreliable.

I understand how difficult it is to maintain this mindset throughout the ups and downs of life. It wasn't until I discovered a coach that it became a clear and almost effortless process. The key to success for Conditionomics couples is that they have sought advice and coaching to show them the way. As a result, they experience an immediate increase in clarity, certainty and resulting confidence. They discover that true confidence comes from understanding your own personal value proposition and implementing simple, affordable strategies to overcome potential dangers. What's more, they share this new found confidence as a couple, which gives them "permission" to do more of the things they value in life sooner – not later.

# CONDITIONOMICS LAW #3

**You will only do more if your confidence in your future increases.**

Let me reemphasize that real security comes from your own skills and abilities, not from any external factors. The clearest understanding I've received about this is from my participation in The Strategic Coach Program by Dan Sullivan, my personal coach. This is where I learned about my Unique Ability* and why I consider this so important in building confidence.

People can and should think of themselves as entrepreneurs, even if someone else currently employs them. Not only is this possible, but in most cases, it's inevitable. We are naturally headed in the direction of a marketplace where people will ultimately be perceived as value creators and others will hire their services. Therefore those of you in the top 15% must understand that the biggest and best investment you can and should make is in your own personal development. Not just in skills training, but investing in the development of your Unique Ability – the thing that you're most passionate about in your work, that energizes you and those around you. Unique Ability is perhaps one of the most profound things that I learned from Dan Sullivan. At first, people struggle to understand it, but once understood, it is incredibly powerful. It validates you as an individual. In simple terms, your Unique Ability consists of the one-to-three activities in your professional life that you absolutely love to do and should therefore be your "work."

---

* TM & © 2005, The Strategic Coach, Inc. All rights reserved. Used with permission. www.strategiccoach.com

That's because the reason you love to do them is you're great at them! It's not self-centered. It's not copping out. It's how you create the most value for yourself and for others and how you will reap the greatest reward. It is also liberating. Once you decide it's OK to develop your Unique Ability, you will stop feeling guilty about doing the things you love to do. The reverse of this is also true. You will never reach your potential or create maximum value UNLESS you are doing what you love to do as a living. Whether it's sewing on buttons, or playing the French horn or tinkering with cars, if you relegate your Unique Ability to a hobby and feel guilty about the time you spend doing that instead of "working" – you will never, by definition, be able to achieve more of the things you want sooner.

Ask someone in their 60s or 70s who, after decades in a corporate job or in the family business, says things like, "I would have loved to be a concert pianist" or "If I'd only started my own flower shop" or "I always wanted to be in radio." They didn't do it because they didn't have the confidence that they could do what they love AND generate a sufficient income to have a great life.

Many people have likened life to a journey. But for the purposes of Law #3, I would like you to think of it more as a process. One of the first steps in the process is discovery. If nothing else, I hope that this book will help you discover the importance of your own Unique Ability and feel the "awakening" of its power to transform not only how you feel about your life, but also what you can do in the time you have on earth. From the day you discover your Unique Ability (see Resource Guide for information on the book "Unique Ability: Creating The Life You Want"), you will begin to feel more confident and become committed to the concept of using it. From that point it only takes a few years to transition from where you are now to where you belong or where you ultimately want to be. The alternative is not pretty. It's discovering that you regret your choices when it's too late to do anything about them. Sadly, you may find yourself not only without financial success and security, but also without relationships that matter and without fulfillment.

The confidence building process takes some time. From the point of discovery, it may take three years to re-engineer your situation and set yourself on the path to your new future. This is a big part of what Conditionomics is about. It is a process of re-conditioning the couple and individuals in preparation for making the major life transitions necessary to achieve Law #2.

# CONDITIONOMICS LAW #4

## Personal freedom and self-determination require financial success.

One of the greatest motivators for people everywhere is greater personal freedom or control over their lives. People also have in common, the desire for personal fulfillment and the need to be valued.

## Money may not buy happiness, but it most certainly buys choices.

In our society, there is a direct correlation between the extent of one's financial resources and the level of personal freedom they can enjoy. Money may not buy happiness, but it most certainly buys choices. Even people who have chosen a seemingly "simpler life" by leaving highly stressful jobs for more service-oriented work and shedding some of their possessions, have been able to do so because at that moment, they have confidence in their future ability to create value (see Conditionomics Law #3). When they do this, however, they are sacrificing some of their ability to make future choices. Conditionomics clients, on the other hand, do not "give up" on the system, but instead, they turn their passion for excellence in all areas into a deeper understanding of how to gain control over their lives.

This is not a selfish philosophy. People who "check out" can't save the world. Only those who become re-energized and direct their energy to fulfill their purpose in life can use their resources for the greater good. People can create more value, be more charitable and help others more if they have more financial resources. This doesn't mean they idolize money. But neither does it mean they depend solely on the "spiritual" to make things better. The people who seem to make the greatest impact, the greatest contributions and help the most people are those who are financially successful and have the attitude: "If it's going to be, it's up to me."

## Financial success is not determined by any specific amount of money.

But what are we talking about when we say "financial success?" Financial success is not determined by any specific amount of money, either in the form of assets or income. It is not measured strictly in numbers. It is defined by three things:

1. Having the ability to earn unlimited (not infinite) income commensurate with the amount of value you create.

2. Having the appropriate allocation of assets and good liabilities (such as low-interest debt that is tax deductible) as determined by the purpose for which those assets were acquired.

3. Having protection against the dangers that could erode or destroy your personal finances, specifically death, disability, lawsuit and taxes.

Like it or not, we live in a culture and a society that requires substantial financial resources if you wish to have personal freedom and self-determination. The people who are most interested in personal freedom and self-determination are the least likely to have a sense of entitlement. They do not expect to be taken care of by someone else, especially not by the government. They are people who understand that to reach financial success they have to create value for others. So it is important for them to figure out how to create that value.

## Obstacles to financial success

Financial success comes in the form of income and assets. Whether they can articulate the reasons or not, everyone would like to be financially successful but most give up because they don't know how to overcome the obstacles to financial success. What are the obstacles?

The first obstacle is our approach to financial decision-making. Most people react to a life event by doing something transactional. For instance, they get married and buy insurance. They have children and create a will. They scrape together a down payment and buy a house. They have extra cash so they buy stocks. These are fragmented and unstructured transactions that make people feel as though they are making progress. But there is no order or structure to such activities.

The second obstacle is the economic system we live in. We live in a society that operates on free enterprise and open competition. While we can appreciate the positive aspects of such a system, we must also realize that by its nature, it creates a barrier to success by encouraging those who represent financial products and services to compete with one another versus collaborating to ensure your absolute best interest.

**One size does not fit all, especially when it comes to how you make, protect and spend your money.**

The third obstacle is misinformation. There are many books (and I've tried very hard to make sure this isn't one of them) that are "how-to," "cookie-cutter" approaches to making financial decisions. These books and articles describe how financial products and services work empirically and on a stand-alone basis as opposed to how they work collectively and uniquely for different individuals. That's because you can't write a book that describes what works for every individual – you can't cover all of the variables. The problem is, the authors of most "how-to" books on financial planning or wealth building present their advice as if it were gospel. People following these sorts of directions may end up making serious mistakes. One size does not fit all, especially when it comes to how you make, protect and spend your money.

The very act of making money does not automatically lead to personal freedom and fulfillment. If it did, everyone who makes a lot of money would be wildly happy and we know that isn't so. Personal freedom comes from doing the things you love to do. Some people misunderstand this. They think they should pursue a high paying profession, regardless of their love for it or lack of love for it, so that eventually they can make enough money to never work again and do only what they love to do. This is a sad myth that has been perpetuated since the California gold rush.

## The key to making a lot of money is to forget about money!

If you do what you love to do, you will make a lot of money. Money follows value creation. Therefore, the key to maximizing your income is to discover what is in your work that you absolutely love to do and focus on doing it to create value for others. These activities will energize you and they will energize the people around you. The discovery of your particular genius – what you love to do – is the key to being impervious to the unreliable structure of Corporate America and attaining the personal freedom and self-fulfillment that everyone seeks. When you discover your Unique Ability and begin to focus on it to create value for others, they will pay you for it and you will begin the transition to the financial success that enables your personal freedom and self-fulfillment.

# CONDITIONOMICS LAW #5

**Financial success requires
special "conditioning."**

Our society does a really good job at conditioning us for academic success and it does a really good job at conditioning us for corporate success. But until now, there has never been a program to condition us to be financially successful.

Ever in search of the perfect solution for financial success, people behave just like serial dieters. Those who are overweight and out of shape are susceptible to every fad diet on the bestseller list. There are perpetual waves of thought about how to lose weight and get fit. And people look for the easiest way to do it. If I stop eating carbs, if I eat only cabbage soup for a month... People spend billions of dollars and read countless books, thirsty for the next best suggestion. The same goes for "getting rich." People look for the silver bullet - the right stock, the right fund, the right insurance, the right kind of mortgage. You can only lose weight one way – eat less, exercise more. The same goes for financial success – get your financial "muscle" into condition by following the process.

It is the purpose in your life that drives you to achieve financial success and most couples do not think about the purpose of their lives, do not define their goals, until they have surplus money. Then they do it only once, as if it were an event. This leads to a limited view of the possibilities.

The "mental muscle" responsible for thinking about your life's purpose and the goals associated with it is unaccustomed to exercise. Like any other muscle in the body, it must be conditioned to function at maximum capacity. Without conditioning, you will never expand your view of the possibilities and never be able to achieve more of the things you value in life sooner rather than later.

Even when couples say they have goals, the goals they state are most often predictable, uninspired and not at all driven by a larger purpose. They are limited because the couple has not been "conditioned" to view possibilities beyond their current or easily attainable ability to fund those goals. Examples of limited, predictable goals are: early retirement, second home on the beach, paying for college for the kids, helping Mom and Dad if they become ill, give more to charity or the church and owning their home free and clear. And how do couples think they're going to do these things? - By sacrificing and making trade-offs now to be able to afford these things.

The special conditioning needed to achieve financial success starts with undoing "bad habits" or breaking through the obstacles to financial success we listed in Conditionomics Law # 4. First the couple has to change their approach to making financial decisions. They have to start making decisions by viewing their effects collectively not just individually. Second, they have to understand that their advisors must collaborate to ensure that their best interests are being served and third, they have to stop allowing themselves to be vulnerable to articles, sales pitches and talk shows. They have to learn how to filter all of that generic "how-to" advice.

Conditionomics coaches help couples integrate and grow their personal, professional and financial lives by teaching and facilitating two things:

1. The cultivation of integrated personal and professional goals

2. The creation and implementation of strategies to achieve those goals

The Conditionomics Coach helps couples cultivate their thinking by facilitating a unique and clearly defined process we call Conditionomics – conditioning the mental muscle to have an expanded view of the possibilities in their lives. This way, purpose-driven goal setting will become an integral part of how a couple makes decisions for the rest of their lives. The Conditionomics Coach's greatest professional legacy is helping couples achieve more of the things they value in life sooner rather than later.

# CONDITIONOMICS LAW #6

**Wealth is not about the money, it is about the purpose for which it is created.**

If you accumulate money by putting your excess in an instrument and leaving it there until you die, what purpose has it served? It has only served your purpose if your purpose in life was to make your children wealthy upon your death. That doesn't sound like a life's purpose that many would knowingly choose. When you think about your legacy, don't you think about your accomplishments, the things you will have done while you were alive? Wouldn't you rather have "posterity" talk about you fondly for the good person you were and the rich and fulfilling life that you led, rather than about the amount of money you left behind? In the end, isn't life really all about making memories?

## Life is all about making memories.

Financial conditioning starts at the beginning of your journey, not at the end. At the beginning is the purpose. It is the first and most important thing to focus on. Only later come the parts of the process that involve wealth accumulation and distribution. These are simple things that enable your purpose to be fulfilled.

If you do things in the right order, defining your purpose and setting your individual and shared goals first, subsequent decisions become much easier to make. Instead of the impulsive way most people are accustomed to making financial decisions that result in a whole collection of inefficient solutions - mutual funds here, CDs there, saving accounts here, stocks and bonds there – you'll have a life-long, "integrated" view of your lives together that will drive purposeful financial decisions.

Here's a typical scenario. 'We need a vacation. What are the best deals? Where can we afford to go? I'll charge it to my credit card. When the bill comes, I'll take money from the easiest source to pay it.' This is not purpose-driven thinking. Once conditioned to focus on the purpose of your life, the decision tree is more like this: 'I'm going to spend quality time with my family in a fun and relaxing environment where everyone's needs can be met and we can make memories together. Which of my funds should I use? My mutual fund prices are high, so instead of reinvesting the dividends, I'll elect to take a cash distribution. Or maybe it's time to sell those stocks that have performed well and take the profit.'

Concentrating on your life's purpose instead of on accumulating money is much more rewarding, much more satisfying, and in the end, will lead you to feel very wealthy indeed.

# CONDITIONOMICS LAW #7

## Wealth is driven by process, not transactions.

Many people believe that the key to financial success is putting their money in the right places at the right time and that success is measured by a high rate of return. Most of us have heard of someone who "made a killing in the stock market" or bought a cheap piece of land that turned out to be worth a mint. But these stories are like tales of the one waitress in a million who gets "discovered" and becomes a movie star or the high school athlete who goes all the way to super stardom. You might as well buy a lottery ticket every day. The act of buying a lottery ticket might make you feel good, but we're all pretty sure that it's not likely to result in financial success.

Action feels good. And in our financial lives, transactions give satisfaction. A classic example is how people fund their children's education. People get a sense of security with a specific type of instrument designed for education such as a 529 plan or Coverdell Education Savings Account (ESA). They are indeed appropriate for some people at some times. But there are other instruments that could be used for the same purpose, perhaps more efficiently with more tax benefit and that accomplish other purposes or goals at the same time. Permanent life insurance is a good example of this because it is tax advantaged, it can provide a fixed interest loan against cash value and at the same time, still afford protection against disability, law suit, creditors and in some instances offer long-term care benefits. The best way to decide these things is to stand up and look at the 'whole dining room table' instead of only at the things on your plate right now.

Wealth creation is best achieved by following a process that is first and foremost driven by purpose and meets multiple goals and objectives all at the same time. The Conditionomics Process™ consists of:

1. Organizing all aspects of your financial life

2. Identifying your most important personal and professional goals and establishing financial objectives to achieve them

3. Evaluating overall efficiency of your current plan as it relates to internal factors (goals and objectives) and external factors (tax laws, market conditions, etc.)

4. Identifying alternatives or options in the form of strategies to achieve more goals sooner with greater certainty

5. Selecting and implementing required/ desired products and services

6. Monitoring and modifying strategies in response to changes in all three areas of your life – resulting in an ever-expanding view of possibilities

The process is never ending – it is ongoing. And there are two dimensions to the process. There is how we go about deciding what is the best thing for us to do based upon our goals and objectives. And there is the other dimension of money.

Conventional thinking dictates that it is best to put money in an instrument and leave it for a long time to offset market volatility. This only works if you have the ability to choose when you're going to take it out. Most people that can choose when they're going to take it out, never need to, so it stays in their estate for their children. In that case, their wealth never served their purpose in life (see Law # 6.)

---

**Money has the ability to work more than one time – to be leveraged.**

---

To understand how money can work more than once imagine that you purchase a home and you put a deposit on that home and take a mortgage on that home – over time creating equity in that home. The purpose for buying the home wasn't necessarily to use it as an investment but rather because owning your home contributes to your quality of life. Homeownership is pleasurable and positively influences your attitude and feelings. Still, by paying your mortgage down and creating equity, you have the ability to leverage that equity by investing in other guaranteed, low-risk instruments or paying for a college education or whatever else serves your life's purpose.

Yes, I agree that it feels good to "do something" instead of only thinking about doing something all the time. However, one of the important tenets of Conditionomics, and the crux of Law #7, is to have patience and respect the process of wealth creation. Why? Because like any game of strategy, if you make your moves too quickly, without playing all the consequences out in your head, you stand to give up your advantages and lose a great deal.

# CONDITIONOMICS LAW #8

## Effective goal setting requires a "change of environment."

Some might say that the greatest value of Conditionomics and The Conditionomics Coach is created very early in the process, at the goal setting stage. Goal setting, or in the language of Conditionomics, **"the goals-driver session"** is a private time when a couple defines the purpose of wealth in their lives.

Though this is often begun in a group setting – the goals are not discussed as a group, only the process of setting the goals is a group activity.

## The most important conversation in your life that you <u>never</u> had

Effective goal setting begins by having what I refer to as "the most important conversation in your life that you never had." This is the conversation between a husband and a wife where they begin to articulate their core ideals, their individual and shared goals and deepest desires. It was probably these things that attracted them to one another in the first place – but amazingly, I have found that most couples have never really spoken the words to each other that confirm their shared purpose. To do this involves thinking "out-of-the-box," which I have found can only be achieved effectively when done outside of your customary setting or environment.

It is humorous to note that without fail, when I ask couples in a goals-driver session the following series of questions about goal setting this is how it goes:

"How many of you believe that setting goals is very important?" Everyone raises his or her hand.

"Do you think it is important to have personal goals?" Everyone says, "Yes."

"Do you think it is important to have professional goals?" Everyone agrees that it is.

"Since everyone agrees, I would like all of you couples to take out your comprehensive lists of individual and shared goals so that we can begin the session." And everyone laughs. Never has a couple brought a comprehensive list of goals to a goals-driver session.

Why is this? Goal setting in other aspects of our lives such as at school or at work is commonplace. But we have never been conditioned to sit down as a couple and set goals together. I believe there are three fundamental barriers to goal setting in our marriages.

1. **We've been conditioned socially to believe that to sit down and make a list of things we want is being selfish.** How can we want for more in this already abundant society

when there are so many people in the world with much less? So we have an immediate sub-conscious aversion to making that list.

2. **It is really hard to set goals.** It was easy as children. We used our imaginations and we were confident that some day we'd get what we wanted. But as adults, the believability factor is missing. We have no reason to believe it's possible, because the cynic in us knows that just closing our eyes and imagining it happening won't really make it happen.

3. **You must get out of your customary environment in order to think about things that are not, but could be.** Where are you going to do goal setting? You have to "get out of box" to think out of the box. Sitting at the kitchen table composing your list of goals results in boilerplate goals that we have been conditioned to believe we want... and nothing beyond. What's more, kitchen table goals are generally individual goals and almost never result in the deep discussion between a husband and a wife necessary to establish shared goals.

Do not underestimate the power of your immediate environment to limit and otherwise negatively influence your thinking.

# CONDITIONOMICS LAW #9

**A fulfilled life is the result
of an ever-expanding
view of possibilities.**

It is difficult to feel optimistic and confident about the future when you can't see beyond the present. Expanding your view of possibilities takes conditioning, just like physical exertion does.

The first time you think about running a 10K, it's daunting and scary. You take your first laps around the neighborhood. You're out of breath very quickly and your shins hurt. You can't imagine feeling stronger, more relaxed. And yet, you know that if you keep at it, it becomes easier and more pleasurable. The goal becomes more and more attainable with each practice run, until finally you can run 10K and beyond. Then it becomes easy to imagine a half-marathon, a marathon and races you may not even know about right now.

Wouldn't it be thrilling and wouldn't it enhance the relationship you have with your spouse, if you knew that the individual and shared goals that you have right now are going to grow beyond what you can even imagine for yourselves today?

Of course, it's a lot easier to get in condition when you're younger. This is true financially as well as physically. The earlier you start the easier it is. When you get financially conditioned early it becomes an energizing part of your life. You will not dread things like paying the bills. You may not enjoy the "exercise" of bill paying, but you will enjoy how it makes you feel.

Paying bills could be a pleasure. 'All the bills are paid and we still have a lot of money in our checkbook. What could we do with it that we would enjoy?' Making car payments to give your children independence or cell phone plans that encourage family members to stay in touch with each other is pleasurable and fulfills a greater purpose.

This is exactly what happens to Conditionomics clients. Couples that follow the process always start out with a limited view of what they can achieve. This is a residual effect of conventional thinking and fear. Initially, they worry about stating goals that seem out of reach. They worry about being disappointed or about disappointing each other if they can't figure out a way to fund those goals. But once they get into steps 3, 4 and 5 of the process as outlined in Law #7, the horizon gets closer and larger and in step 6 of the process, couples begin to have a much more expansive view of the possibilities.

Throughout the process, couples begin to communicate differently. They are more positive, more open, more focused on success. Conditionomics couples also feel differently about their future. They are more confident and more purposeful about their personal, professional and financial lives. And they understand that all three are interdependent. They understand that wealth is created in their professional lives, protected in their financial lives and put to use for their purposes in their personal lives. And it is in their personal lives that their view of possibilities begins and continues to expand. There is nothing more fulfilling than believing that you have not, and probably never will reach the limits of what you can do with your life.

# CONDITIONOMICS LAW #10

**The easiest and most enjoyable way to realize your potential is with the guidance of a skilled coach.**

To use the health and fitness analogy again, it is more effective, more fun and more motivating to work out with a personal trainer than it is to do it on your own. First of all, a certified personal trainer is a professional who is an expert in human physiology, nutrition and equipment. The trainer will show you the way and help you avoid injury and wasted energy. Of course, the trainer can't do it for you – you have to do the work yourself and you have to decide on your own goals and objectives as well as how you will measure success.

In the Conditionomics Process, the Conditionomics coach helps individuals and couples believe they will achieve their goals by developing strategies for doing so.

Conditionomics Coaches, all skilled, experienced financial service professionals, are uniquely qualified to understand and facilitate the integration of your personal, professional and financial lives. They are the ones who have the ability; more than any other, to facilitate that "most important conversation that the couple never had" – the one about individual and shared goals. They can help eliminate the myths that both society and the financial industry have perpetuated over the years. They can help increase the couple's certainty of future outcomes so that their view of possibilities will expand and grow. It is the job of the licensed and trained Conditionomics Coach to remind you that there are no financial goals; there are only personal and professional goals, which are supported by financial objectives and resulting strategies.

Guided by a Conditionomics Coach, not only will planning your future with your spouse be more fun and more productive, you will soon begin to see the changes you can make right now – and make them! You will have the things that are important to you sooner, rather than later. And you will begin to believe your view of possibilities will be ever-expanding.

# CONCLUSION

Back in the beginning of this book, I asserted that many of us would live to be 100 years old. If you believe that you will live to be 100, you should stop focusing on the financial legacy you will leave your children and start focusing on the values-based, goals-driven purpose of your life. Why? Because if you live to be 100, the money you'll leave your children won't make much of a difference in their lives at age 70 or so. They are not likely to need your money – but they could benefit greatly if the legacy you leave consists of the principles behind Conditionomics and the encouragement to create value in the world through their own Unique Abilities.

## Will you be able to take advantage of opportunities when they come along?

I hope you and perhaps your spouse have enjoyed this book and that it has introduced concepts to you that you find interesting and inspiring. If you want to increase the value you as an individual and the two of you as a couple bring to this life – and do it forever – the key is to understand how your personal, professional and financial lives are integrated. If you internalize the 10 Laws of Conditionomics, you will easily generate enough wealth to take advantage of opportunities when they come along, provide for the dangers that threaten your resources and enhance your future-focused relationship with your spouse and the rest of your family. I can assure you that even the most forward-thinking of you has a much more limited view of possibilities than you will have just three years from now...if you change your thinking.


If the ideas contained in this book have intrigued you and left you wanting to know more or think further about Conditionomics, we invite you visit www. conditionomics.com

# ABOUT CONDITIONOMICS

Conditionomics is a unique wealth coaching methodology that not only changes the way you think about money, but more importantly, it will help you clarify its purpose in your life and dramatically expand your view of possibilities.

Conditionomics is categorically different than any other kind of advising you have ever received. I would venture to guess that no other financial planner, accountant, legal advisor, or counselor of any sort that you have ever had, has taken an integrated approach to your personal, professional and financial life. I would also guess that no advisor has worked with you and your spouse as a couple to the extent that the two of you have grown closer emotionally and begun to plan your future together with great excitement and on a regular basis.

# A FEW WORDS ABOUT COUPLES

As I've noted elsewhere in this book, we at Conditionomics are always surprised to learn how little many couples share with each other about what's really important in life – even couples who have been married for twenty years and more.

This is why I say that a Conditionomics Coach can facilitate you and your spouse "having the most important conversation that you never had."

Now we don't claim to be marriage counselors. Interestingly though, a number of Conditionomics clients have told us that while they came to us for coaching about financial matters, they walked away with some added value that was totally unexpected. They walked away with an enlightened perspective on what really matters to their spouse and a new confidence that, as a couple, they could masterfully integrate their personal, professional and financial lives. Learning this has only reinforced for me how powerful the 10 Laws of Conditionomics can really be.

# Resource Guide

## RECOMMENDED READING

1.  *Unique Ability: Creating The Life You Want* by Catherine Nomura and Julia Waller. Toronto, Ontario: The Strategic Coach Inc., 2003.

2.  *The Great Crossover* by Dan Sullivan. Toronto, Ontario: The Strategic Coach Inc., 2000.

3.  *Today Matters* by John C. Maxwell. New York, NY: Warner Faith, 2004.

4.  *Thinking For A Change* by John C. Maxwell. New York, NY: Warner Books, Inc., 2003.

5.  *The Power of Focus* by Jack Canfield, Mark Victor Hansen and Les Hewitt. Deerfield Beach, FL: Health Communications, Inc., 2000.

6.  *One Small Step Can Change Your Life The Kaizen Way* by Robert Maurer, Ph.D. New York, NY: Workman Publishing Company, Inc., 2004.

7.  *Managing In The Next Society* by Peter F. Drucker. New York, NY: Truman Talley Books, 2002.

8.  *The Experience Economy* by Joseph Pine II and James H. Gilmore. Boston, MA: Harvard Business School Press, 1999.

9.  *Rich Dad's Who Took My Money?* By Robert T. Kiyosaki and Sharon L. Lechter. New York, NY: Warner Books, 2004.

10. *The Parent Care Solution* by Dan Taylor. Bloomington, IN: AuthorHouse, 2004.

# AUDIO TAPES

11. *The Goal Cultivator Series* by Dan Sullivan. The Strategic Coach Inc. Toronto, Ontario. 800-387-3206

12. *Always Increase Your Confidence Series* by Dan Sullivan. The Strategic Coach Inc. Toronto, Ontario. 800-387-3206

13. *Learning How To Avoid The Gap* by Dan Sullivan. The Strategic Coach Inc. Toronto, Ontario. 800-387-3206

14. *Awaken The Giant Within* by Anthony Robbins. San Diego, California: Robbins Research International. 800-898-8669

# COURSES

## Personal Financial Coaching

15. The Conditionomics Coach Program. Toll free: 866-921-0701.
    www.conditionomics.com

## Business Coaching

16. The Strategic Coach Program. Toll free: 800-387-3206
    Canada: 416-531-7399 U.S.A.: 847-699-5767
    www.strategiccoach.com

# PERSONALITY PROFILES

17. Kolbe Concepts Inc. Phoenix, Arizona. 602-840-9770
    www.kolbe.com

# ABOUT THE AUTHOR

Michael A. Campbell is the creator and President of The Conditionomics Coach, LLC. He is a professional entrepreneur, a mentor and a personal wealth coach. He has an uncanny ability to instill confidence by simplifying complex matters in a way that moves people, especially married couples, to take positive action. He inspires couples by enabling them to expand their view of possibilities to do more of the things they value in life, sooner rather than later. One of Michael's favorite tasks is to encourage his married couple clients to "Have the most important conversation in their lives, that they've never had."